EASIEST 5-FINGER PIANO COLLECTION

GW00368198

Film Songs

15 popular film songs arranged for 5-finger piano

Wise Publications
part of The Music Sales Group
London / New York / Paris / Sydney / Copenhagen / Berlin / Madrid / Tokyo

EDELWEISS

Words by Oscar Hammerstein II. Music by Richard Rodgers.

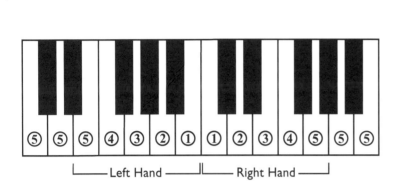

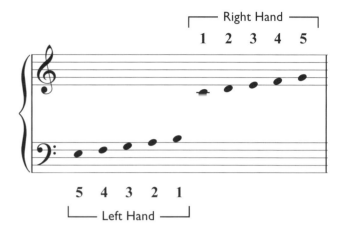

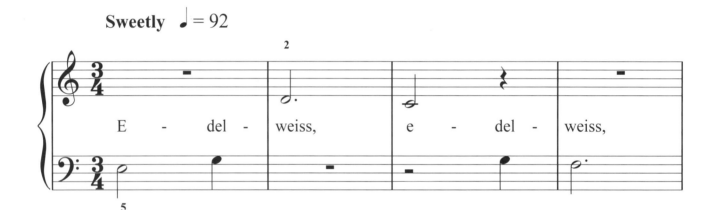

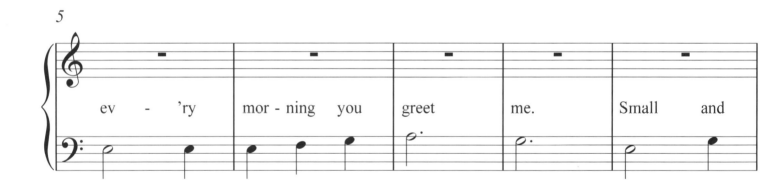

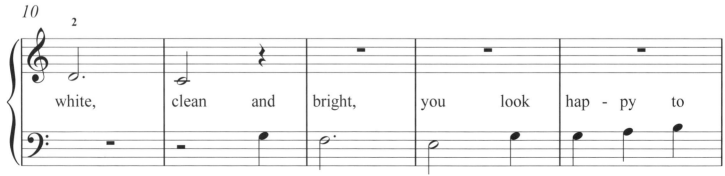

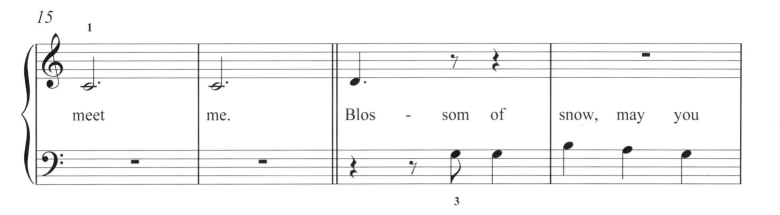

meet me. Blos - som of snow, may you

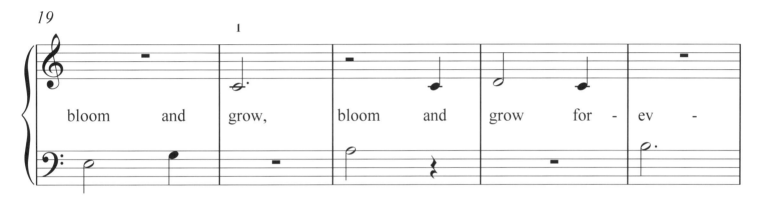

bloom and grow, bloom and grow for - ev -

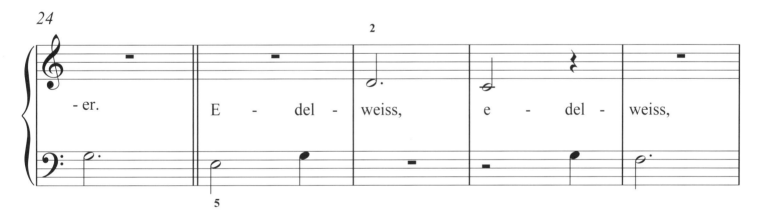

- er. E - del - weiss, e - del - weiss,

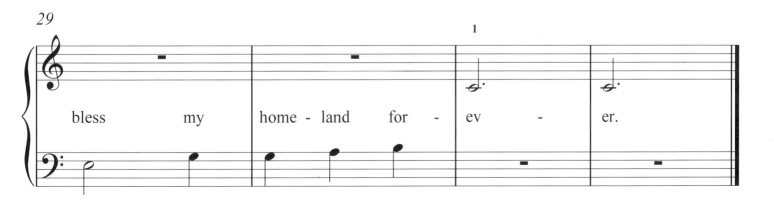

bless my home - land for - ev - er.

RULE THE WORLD

Words & Music by Mark Owen, Gary Barlow, Jason Orange & Howard Donald

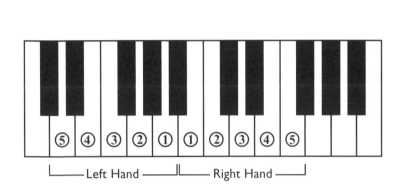

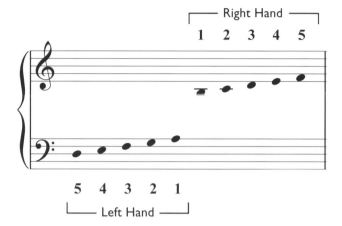

Steadily, with a strong beat ♩ = 82

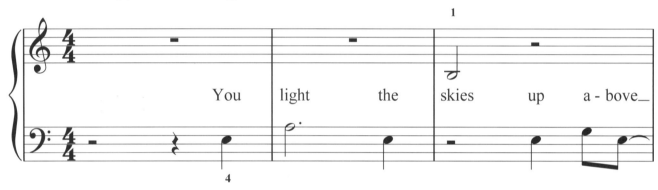

You light the skies up a-bove

— me, a star so bright you blind—

— me, yeah. Don't close your eyes, don't fade a-way,—

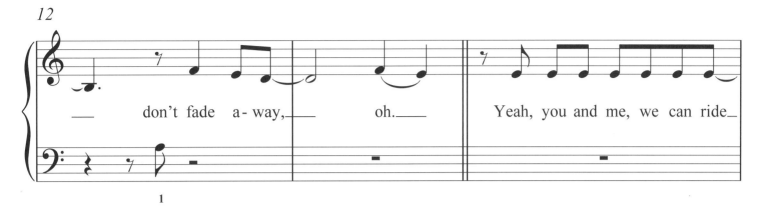

WHO WILL BUY?

Words & Music by Lionel Bart

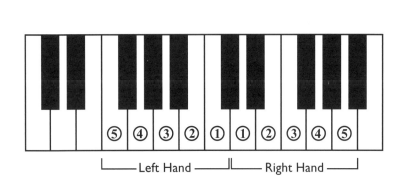 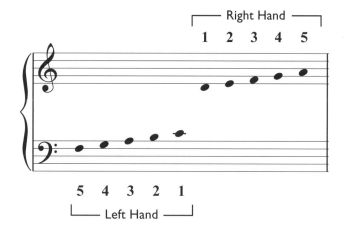

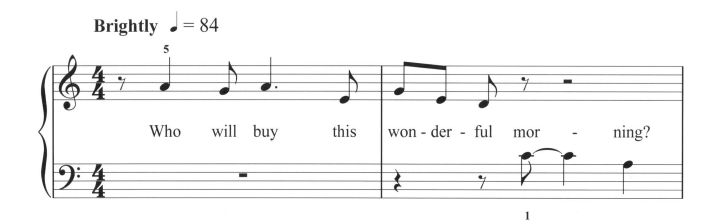

Who will buy this won-der-ful mor-ning?

Such a sky, you nev-er did see.___ Who will tie it

up with a rib-bon, and put it in a box for me.

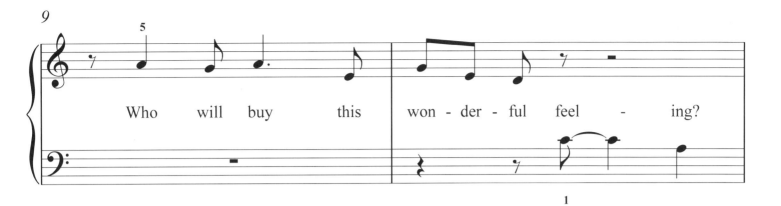

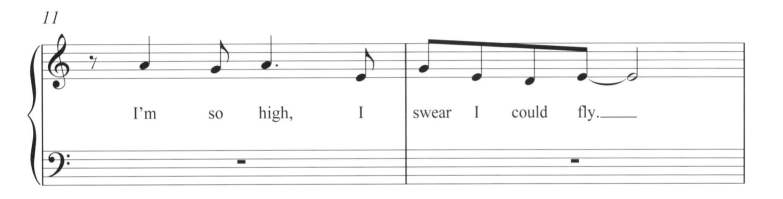

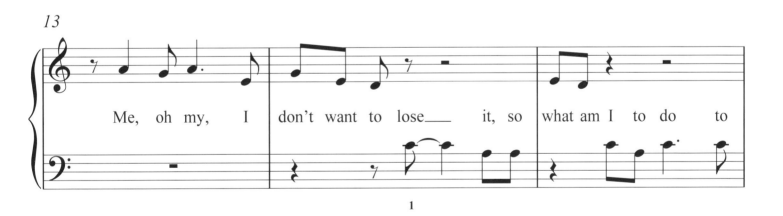

THE CANDY MAN

Words & Music by Leslie Bricusse & Anthony Newley

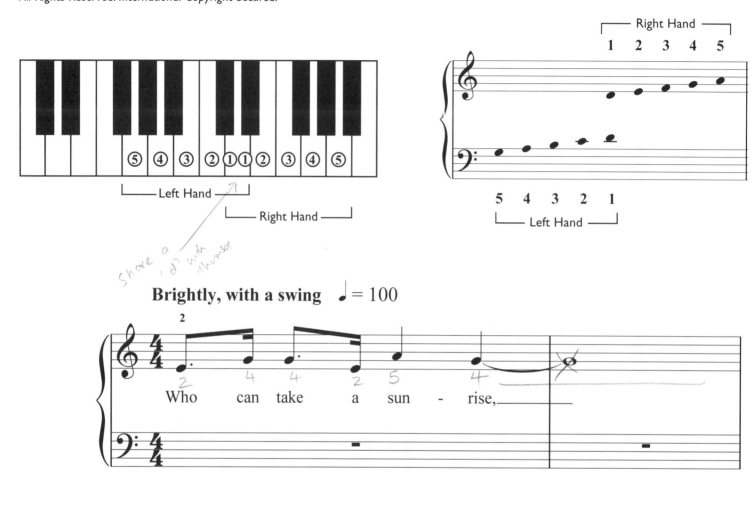

Brightly, with a swing ♩ = 100

Who can take a sun - rise,

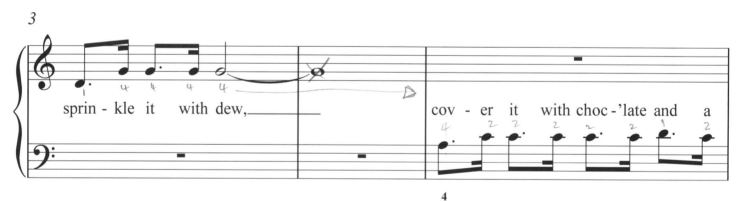

sprin - kle it with dew,_____ cov - er it with choc -'late and a

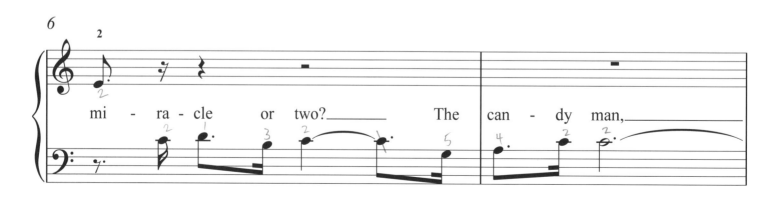

mi - ra - cle or two?_____ The can - dy man,_____

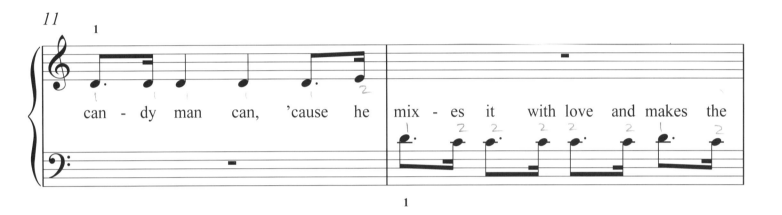

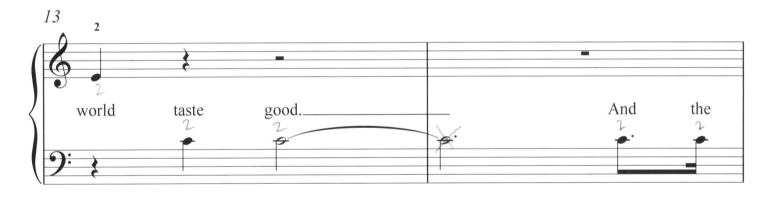

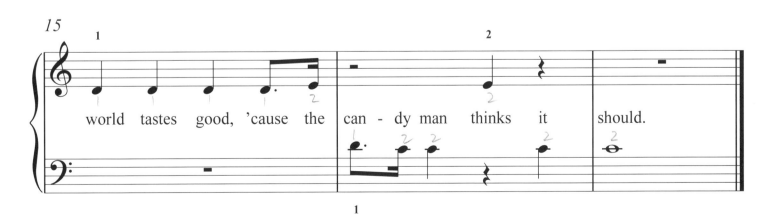

A WHOLE NEW WORLD

Music by Alan Menken. Words by Tim Rice

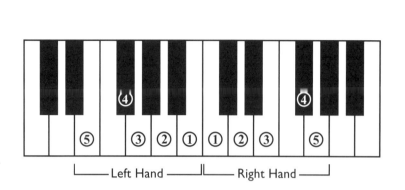

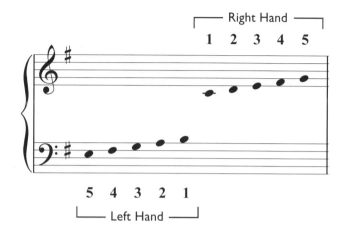

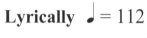

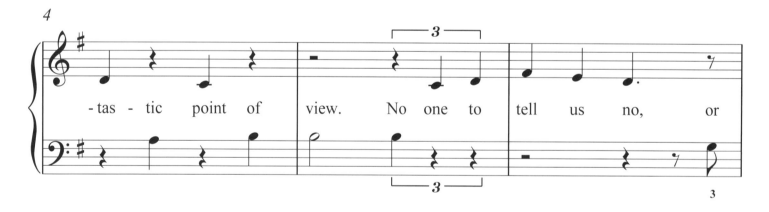

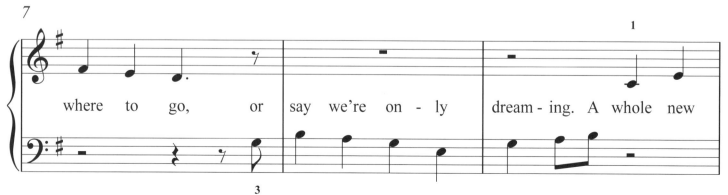

I'M A BELIEVER

Words & Music by Neil Diamond

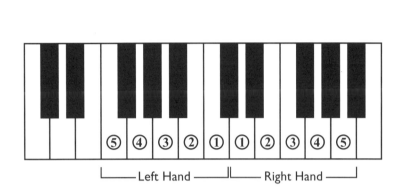

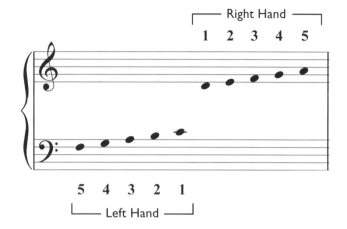

With confidence ♩ = 80

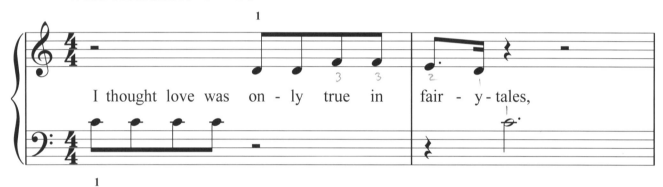

I thought love was on-ly true in fair-y-tales,

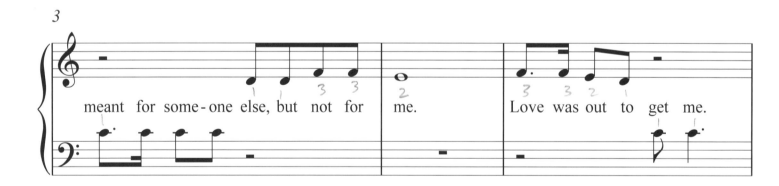

meant for some-one else, but not for me. Love was out to get me.

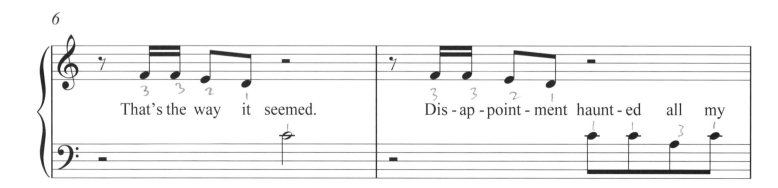

That's the way it seemed. Dis-ap-point-ment haunt-ed all my

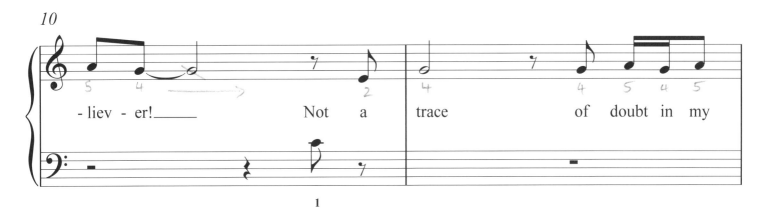

ORDINARY MIRACLE

Words & Music by Glen Ballard & Dave Stewart

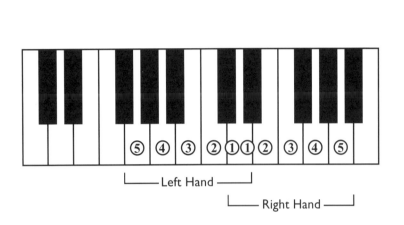

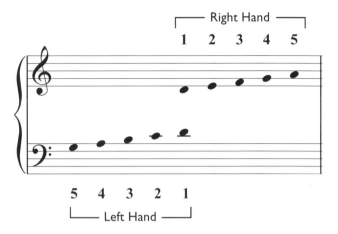

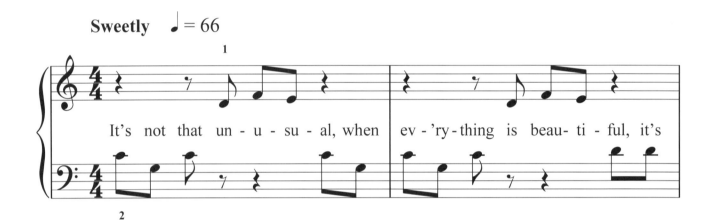

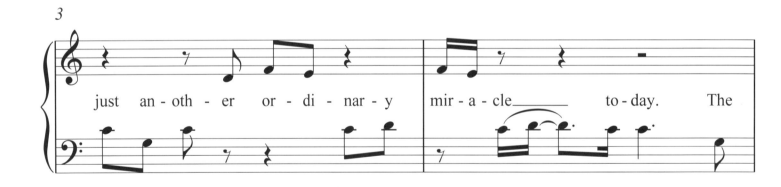

YOU'VE GOT A FRIEND IN ME

Words & Music by Randy Newman

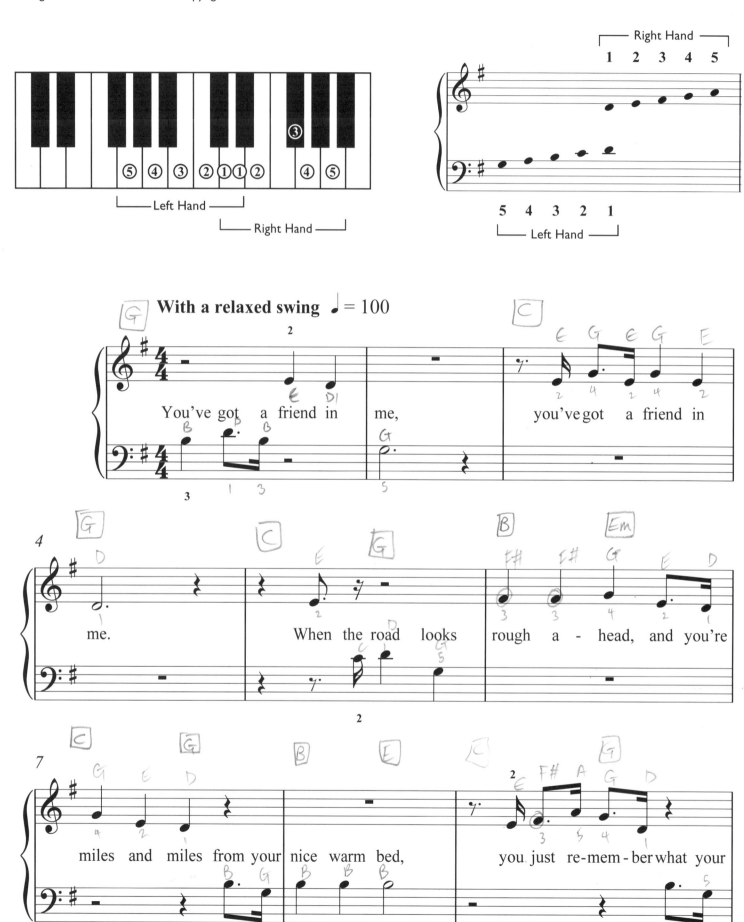

BREAKING FREE

Words & Music by Jamie Houston

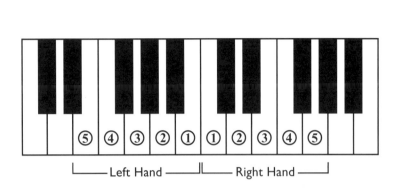

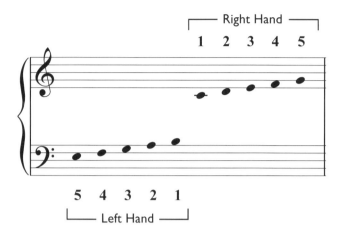

With confidence ♩ = 108

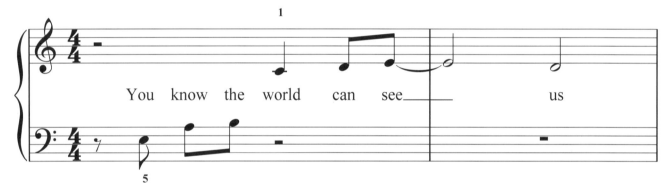

You know the world can see___ us

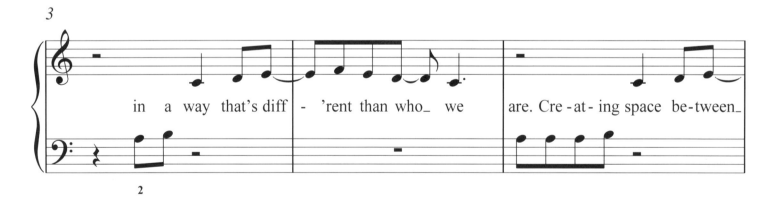

in a way that's diff - 'rent than who_ we are. Cre -at - ing space be-tween_

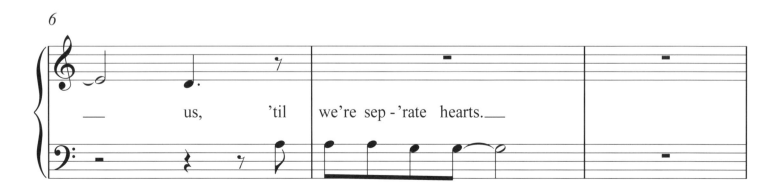

___ us, 'til we're sep -'rate hearts.___

DON'T WORRY, BE HAPPY

Words & Music by Bobby McFerrin

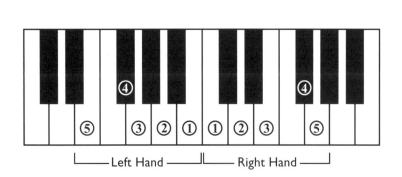

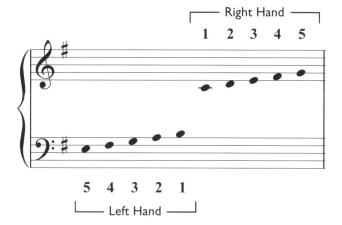

With a relaxed swing ♩ = 112

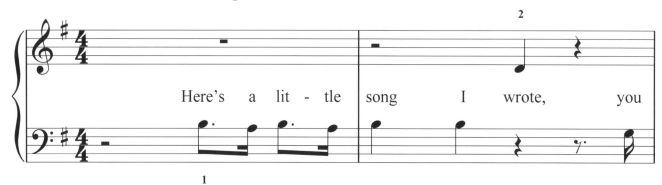

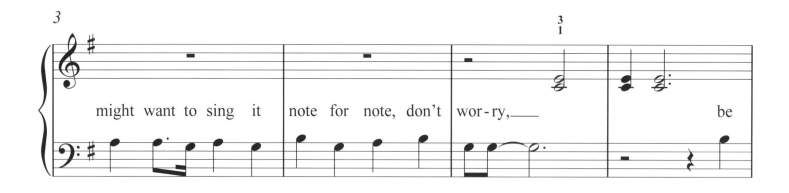

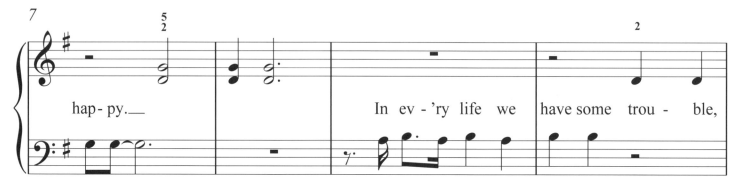

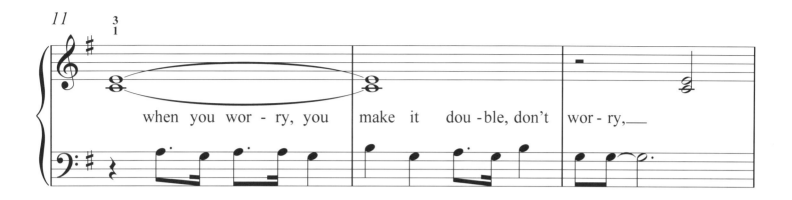

when you wor - ry, you make it dou -ble, don't wor - ry,___

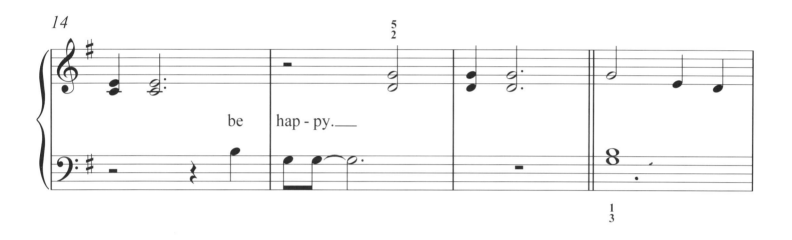

be hap - py.___

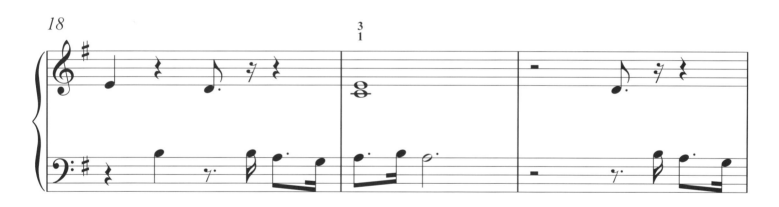

THE BEST DAY EVER

Words & Music by Tom Kenny & Andy Paley

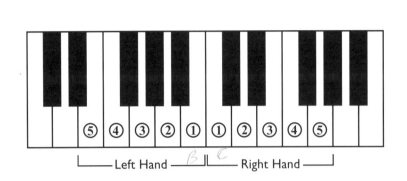

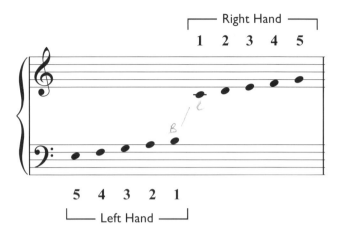

Happily, with a swing ♩ = 126

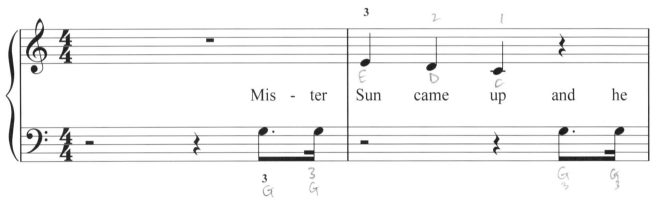

Mis - ter Sun came up and he

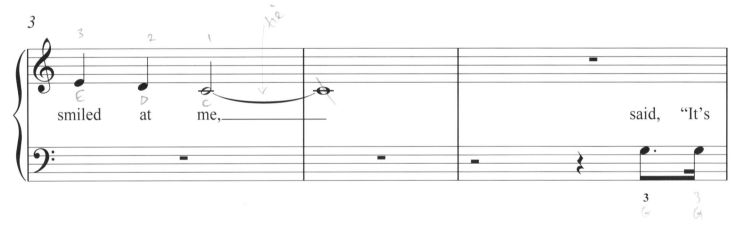

smiled at me, said, "It's

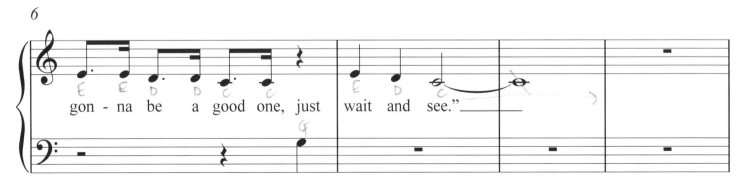

gon - na be a good one, just wait and see." ___

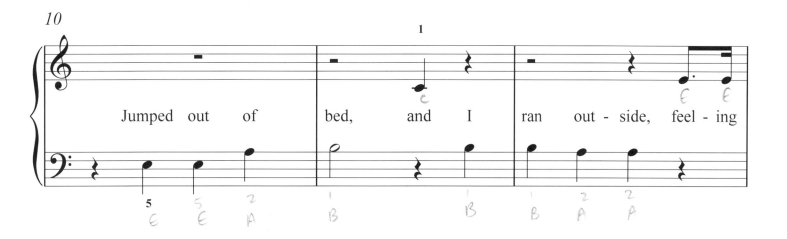

Jumped out of bed, and I ran out-side, feel-ing

so ex - tra ec - sta - ti - fied! It's the best day

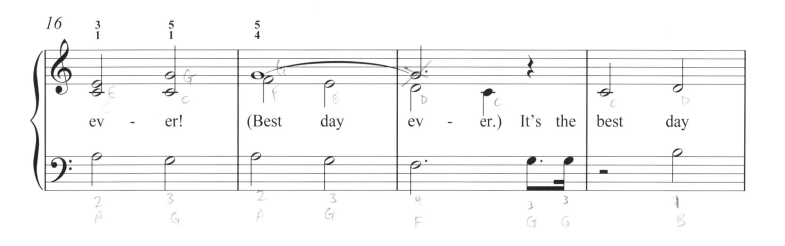

ev - er! (Best day ev - er.) It's the best day

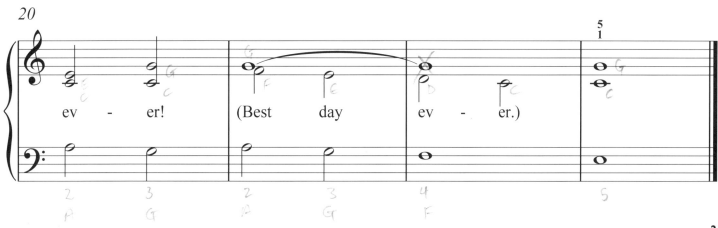

ev - er! (Best day ev - er.)

SOMEWHERE OUT THERE

Words & Music by James Horner, Barry Mann & Cynthia Weil

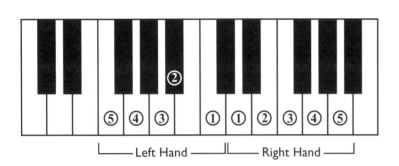

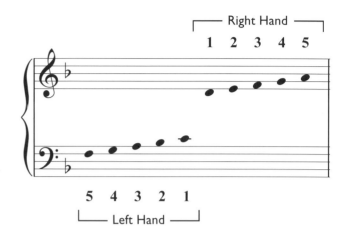

Expressively ♩ = 80

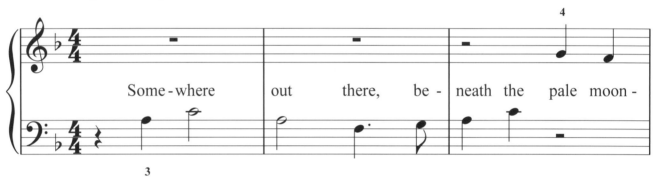

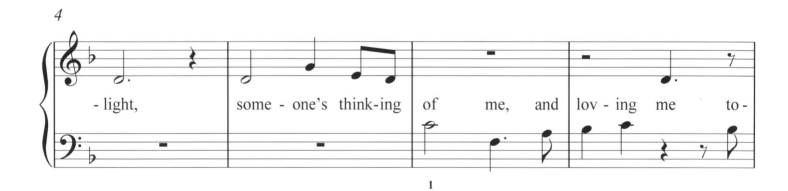

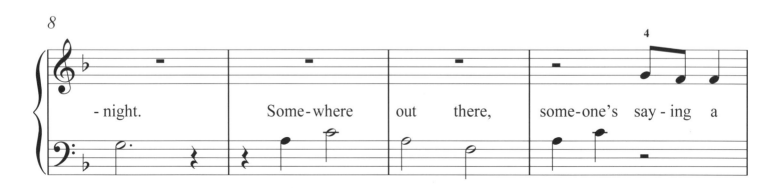

prayer, that we'll find one an- oth - er in that

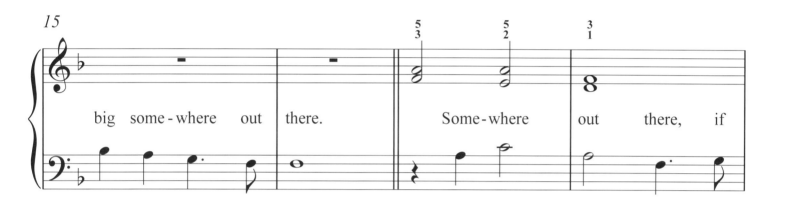

big some-where out there. Some-where out there, if

love can see us through, then we'll be to- geth - er, some-where

out there, out where dreams come true.

SUPER TROUPER

Words & Music by Benny Andersson & Björn Ulvaeus

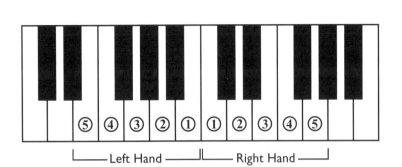

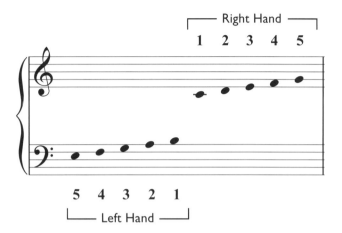

Briskly ♩ = 112

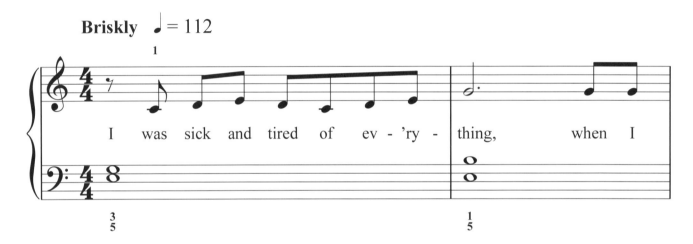

I was sick and tired of ev-'ry - thing, when I

called you last night from Glas - gow. All I do is eat and sleep and

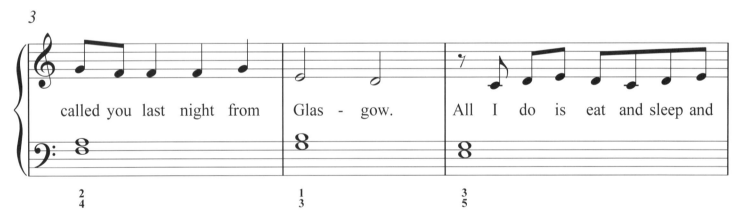

sing, wish-ing ev-'ry show was the last show.

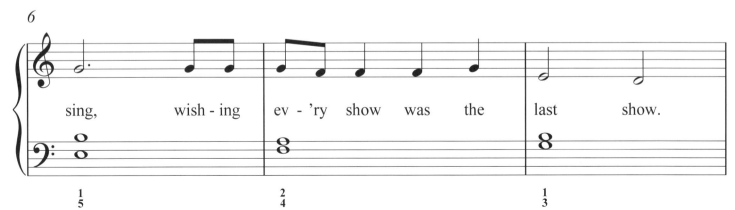

BOOGIE WONDERLAND

Words & Music by Jon Lind & Allee Willis

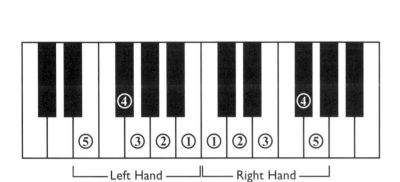

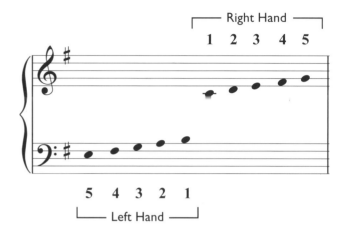

Briskly and rhythmically ♩ = 126

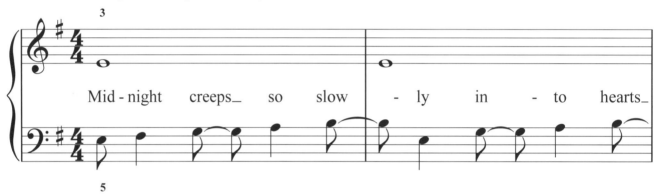

Mid-night creeps so slow- ly in-to hearts

_ of men_ who need_ more than_ they get. Day-light deals a bad

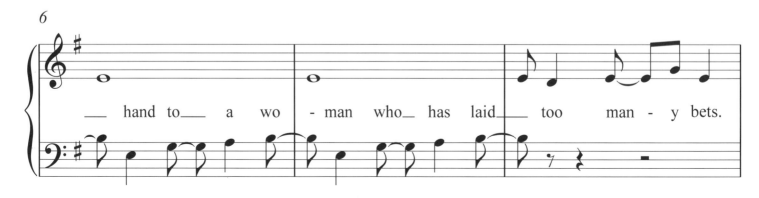

_ hand to _ a wo- man who_ has laid_ too man-y bets.

I BELIEVE I CAN FLY

Words & Music by R. Kelly

EASIEST 5-FINGER PIANO COLLECTION

ALSO AVAILABLE IN THE SERIES!

Ballads
A superb collection of 15 well-known ballads, including 'Fix You', 'I Have A Dream', 'Let It Be' and 'What A Wonderful World'.
AM995346

Chart Hits
15 popular chart hits including 'About You Now', 'Bleeding Love', 'Clocks', 'Foundations', 'Shine' and 'Umbrella'.
AM995357

Showtunes
15 great showtunes including 'Any Dream Will Do', 'Circle Of Life', 'Mamma Mia' and 'My Favourite Things'.
AM995324

Download to your computer a set of piano accompaniments for this *Film Songs* edition
(to be played by a teacher/parent).
Visit: **www.hybridpublications.com**
Registration is free and easy.
Your registration code is TF234

Published by
Wise Publications
14-15 Berners Street,
London W1T 3LJ, UK.

Exclusive Distributors:
Music Sales Limited
Distribution Centre, Newmarket Road,
Bury St Edmunds, Suffolk IP33 3YB, UK.
Music Sales Pty Limited
20 Resolution Drive, Caringbah,
NSW 2229, Australia.

Order No. AM995335
ISBN 978-1-84772-725-1

Edited by Fiona Bolton.
Arranging and engraving supplied by Camden Music.

Printed in the EU.

Your Guarantee of Quality
As publishers, we strive to produce every
book to the highest commercial standards.
This book has been carefully designed to
minimise awkward page turns and to
make playing from it a real pleasure.
Particular care has been given to specifying acid-free,
neutral-sized paper made from pulps which have
not been elemental chlorine bleached.
This pulp is from farmed sustainable forests and was
produced with special regard for the environment.
Throughout, the printing and binding have been
planned to ensure a sturdy, attractive publication
which should give years of enjoyment.
If your copy fails to meet our high standards,
please inform us and we will gladly replace it.

www.musicsales.com